The Circle

The Circle

by David Lloyd

A HAIKU SEQUENCE ————

———— WITH ILLUSTRATIONS

CHARLES E. TUTTLE COMPANY

Rutland • Vermont & Tokyo • Japan

REPRESENTATIVES
Continental Europe: BOXERBOOKS, INC., Zurich
British Isles: PRENTICE-HALL INTERNATIONAL, INC., London
Australasia: PAUL FLESCH & CO., PTY. LTD., Melbourne
Canada: HURTIG PUBLISHERS, Edmonton

Published by the Charles E. Tuttle Company, Inc.
of Rutland, Vermont & Tokyo, Japan
with editorial offices at
Suido 1-chome, 2-6, Bunkyo-ku, Tokyo

Copyright in Japan, 1974
by Charles E. Tuttle Co., Inc.

Library of Congress Catalog Card No. 74-77264
International Standard Book No. 0-8048 1138-5

First printing, 1974

Printed in Japan

This book is dedicated
to all those who have taught me and
all those that I have been honored to teach;
especially it is for the
Madonna of the Roses

Preface

FOR ME THERE ARE NINE JOYS CONNECTED WITH THIS first book of haiku and sketches. The primary joy concerns my home and children. Without this environment to share, explore, discover, and grow in, there would have been no poems, no music, no circle.

Secondly, without the editors of the haiku magazines in America and elsewhere, no book could have been written. So my deepest thanks go to Eric Amann and William J. Higginson of *Haiku Magazine*, Jean Calkins of the former *Haiku Highlights*, Leroy Kanterman of *Haiku West*, Kay Titus Mormino of *Modern Haiku*, Lorraine E. Harr of *Dragonfly*, Gerry Loose of *Haiku Byways* in England, Janice M. Bostok of *Tweed* in Australia, and to all others who have guided, scolded, corrected, and printed some of these haiku.

A third joy is the opportunity to pay two men some great debts. To Harold Henderson must go the most since it is his guide and love song to Japan called *Introduction to Haiku* that nurtured my first fumbling efforts. And to R. H. Blyth's work goes thanks for the scholarship and the dedication and the knowledge he has passed down with such love and care.

My fourth joy is in Nature herself. In this book and in all my own haiku, one attempts to learn from the vastness that is there. Like some backyard Thoreau, each of us can benefit from knowing one small place better and more thoroughly. For me, this place is our yard. Yet this yard also extends outward to my town, Pitman, my county, Gloucester, my state, New Jersey, my country the United States, my world, this earth. And since there is not any one point where that begins or ends, it is my circle, my joy in the endless search to tell its tales, its songs, and find its meanings no matter how skillfully or clumsily.

A fifth joy comes from the haiku that others have written. Besides the haiku that come from the world as it is observed, there are moments sent to us—little hunks of *now*—and we respond to these not just to imitate or adapt but to pay a kind of tribute and a kind of thanks and to point a finger. Each haiku writer owes every other haiku writer in some way.

A sixth joy comes from the mystery. Call it Zen or call it Christianity or call it Nature—it is there. In each or from each comes the search. From each and in each, one may learn a way. One part of that way says that what we call heaven is within. And if so, then within each haiku is a piece of that heaven. Some may accept each piece; others may accept some; and still others may reject it all. But through haiku one may know it is there inside of everything waiting to be discovered, realized, searched for, and conveyed to others if they will share that circle.

Now the seventh joy concerns our time, the era which we have been born into. As you know, many curse our time, but for me it is all I know. And in this time, haiku have been more varied and experimental in English than, perhaps, in any other period. This frees me from the usual 5/7/5 interpretation or definition. Despite that freedom, you will find many haiku that follow the pattern and when there is deviation, it is usually within R. H. Blyth's suggestion for using a shorter line followed by a longer line followed by a shorter line. This flow or beat or wave is used not only for the sake of a discipline but also for a sense of joy in patterns.

My eighth joy concerns other techniques of the haiku supplied by our time as well. For example, you will find ample use of strong comparisons and/or contrasts;

you will discover attempts at objective reports; there are haiku based upon a faith in what others might call small or insignificant things. And there are haiku about merging, mutability, the tiny and the great, a thing and its essence, man and the vast, self-portrayals, humanity in nature and nature in humanity, and attempts at humor. Seasonal images are used. Sensations are explored. "Suchness" is sought.

The ninth and last joy is this book itself and the publisher, Charles E. Tuttle, who is making it possible. Despite our attempts to be modest or humble, one is still proud to be singled out in some way. I only hope that this book of early and clumsy efforts and beginnings in the haiku form finds some reader who will take them into his circle of being.

—DAVID LLOYD

The Haiku

Now thrown back
Into the surge of the surf,
The melting mists.

During the thaw,
  Rising bubbles within bubbles
  Still bubbling . . .

Modern Haiku
Vol. II, No. 2

The ink quill splitting
And spattering the paper
This cold spring evening . . .

Modern Haiku
Vol. II, No. 2

Still cutting up
    The cold March moon,
        Bare, black branches . . .

The last in fall,
    And now the first in spring:
    Green willow leaves.

On the bare floor,
  In the middle of March,
    A brown shield-bug.

Finding the broom
   In the corner of the garage
     And a few spiders.

Melting
  Back into the mists,
   Forsythia.

Almost faceless
In the pounding showers,
A pale pansy.

Haiku Byways
Vol. I, No. 3

Lying on the lawn
  A pile of picked dandelions
  And a drunken man.

Sitting down,
    And staying to watch them close—
    White bloodroot blossoms . . .

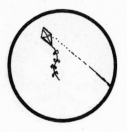

The yellow kite:
  Shining way up in the sky—
  The boy shining too.

Getting up again
  To look at cherry blossoms
    In the moonlight.

First the blossoms,
Then the cherries,
Now the leaves . . .

Haiku Magazine
Vol. IV, No. 2/3

Tender bamboo shoots
Growing up and away from
The old bamboo tree.

Flowing downstream
  Between the mountain pines,
  A bird's embryo.

Haiku Magazine
Vol. IV, No. 2/3

Dogwood blossoms,
Their edges turning brown
Recalling legends.

Holding it close
 So it looks bigger than it is—
  The first mayapple

Modern Haiku
Vol. II, No. 2

From the boat
    Seeing the baby whale
        And the mother's eye.

Little red ants
  Climbing up the peonies—
    My eyes too.

The rake
  Repeating itself
    In the dark, wet ground.

The car's lights
Picking out night bloomers
In the driveway.

In the field—
Even before school's out—
These wild daisies.

Blinded
  From the sunflowers—
    Still staring . . .

Haiku Magazine
Vol. 5, No. 1
First version

With one's mind
Knowing the blueberry;
And with the mouth!

Haiku Magazine
Vol. IV, No. 2/3

Brown hands
 Turning purple
  From blackberries.

Wild rose bending—
And bending even more
With the bee's weight.

The ink drawing
  Not looking like a flower
    Till the sun hits it.

The ladybug
Not listening
  To the song . . .

Haiku Highlights
Vol. VIII, No. 4

This pale petal,
From the rose blossom
Is heart-shaped.

With the noon whistle,
  The blue jay hangs upside down
    For sunflower seeds.

At sixty
  He listens to roses
    With obedient ears.

Haiku Byways
Vol. I, No. 2

Tapping again
  On the back screen door,
    A June bug.

All over town
  Only the noon whistle
    And cicada-talk.

On the oak tree—
This July the fourth—
Two red leaves.

Orange blossoms
In the blue-black sky :
The fireworks.

Monarch butterfly
Softly flutters by
Queen Anne's lace.

Hearing the storm tide:
  Walking the water line in rain—
    Touched by more than rain . . .

The seagulls
　　Not taking from my hands
　　　Their daily bread . . .

Haiku Byways
Vol. I, No. 2

Sharing the beach
While sitting on my knuckle,
This sand flea . . .

Coming slowly
Down the glass at noon,
A lightning bug . . .

Haiku Magazine
Vol. V, No. 2

The mosquito
Filling up with blood
And a full moon!

Haiku Magazine
Vol. IV, No. 2/3

Day lilies:
Actually closed
Tonight.

Perfectly still
  Under the wavering myrtle,
    A tiny toad.

Summer vacation
In Japan—learning to tie
A fivefold gift-knot.

A rooster crowing
  While we are passing through
    The torii gates . . .

Below the sharp points,
A soft pine needle bed
And the smell of it.

While on vacation,
Forgetting the chilly wind—
Watching Fujisan.

Perfectly still
On the marigold,
A bumblebee.

Within themselves,
On top of themselves,
Lichens spreading . . .

Haiku Byways
Vol. I, No. 3

Stepping on
The beginning
Of autumn . . .

An Adaptation
From a lost source

Come too late
  For the cucumbers
    You moral bug?

Greening again
  In September's cool,
    The grasses . . .

In and out
 Of blue blossoms,
  Flying ants.

Modern Haiku
Vol. II, No. 1

First announcing spring
And now announcing fall,
Yellow dandelions.

Inside the red,
  Some green; inside the green,
    Some red . . .

Now gently holding
In the hollow of my hand
Tomorrow's oak tree . . .

Haiku West
Vol. VI, No. 1

Ducks in the sky
Beginning to leave their prints
Beneath the gingko.

The yellowjack's wings
Making the warm air cooler
By the red clover.

Startled up
  From the lawn by the Peke,
    This webworm moth . . .

Over dried grass,
Two butterflies—
And a chill wind . . .

Haiku Magazine
Vol. IV, No. 2/3

The bright thistles
Inviting hummingbirds
Past the sharp points.

Seeing our neighbor's
  Red dogwood berries, and then
    Noticing our own.

Twigs fall,
Leaves are rustling,
Ants come in.

Haiku Byways
Vol. I, No. 2

Bent over
   With the barley heads,
   An old man.

Duck feathers
  On the lake's shore—
    Silent skies.

Haiku Magazine
Vol. IV, No. 2/3

All through the night,
Oak leaves skittering,
And skittering.

Trying to recall
Dogwood blossoms
As leaves fall.

Haiku Byways
Vol. I, No. 2

Brown and withering
  Yet still alive and whispering,
    The wind swept grasses.

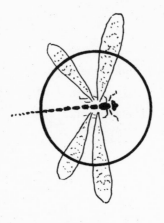

Dead dragonfly:
The wings moving—
Not moving.

Haiku Magazine
Vol. IV, No. 2/3

Paper birch pods
Dropping into the empty
Canoe . . .

One by one
In the autumn wind,
Thistledown . . .

Haiku Byways
Vol. I, No. 2

Wisteria
  Still trying to strangle
    The wire . . .

Taking leaves
From my yard to your yard,
Autumn winds . . .

Haiku Magazine
Vol. IV, No. 4

Large white flakes
Landing on the red maple
And melting.

Adapted from
original version in
The Windless Orchard
Vol. I, No. 4

Holding this seed
On Thanksgiving day—
Now letting it go.

The laughing children
  Taking the brown leaves in hand
  And stripping them . . .

The acorn
 Casts a long shadow
  On the dry leaves . . .

On the tip
 Of each cold azalea leaf,
  A small white point . . .

Modern Haiku
Vol. II, No. 1

Watching winter rain
And the ripples bumping,
Bumping, bumping . . .

Heaps
  Of dead clam shells,
    And one snail's . . .

First scolding the spring
And now scolding the winter,
A brassy blue jay.

Opening my mouth
    And dancing about beneath
        The first snowflakes.

Also arriving
  With the large, wet snowflakes,
  A final flower . . .

Slowly growing
On the old fence post,
A small snow pile.

The snowballs
Now clinging to each other
In the sudden cold.

Only this one
  Very small hump of snow
  Resisting the sun.

Wavering by
  On this sunny winter day,
    A bumble bee . . .

Modern Haiku
Vol. II, No. 1

See the sharp needles
Forever sewing the sky
To the pine branches.

Haiku Highlights
Vol. VI. No. 5

The earth all gone
  The sky all gone and still
    The snow comes down.

Modern Haiku
Vol. II, No. 3
Adapted from Shiki

The chirping bird
  Barely disturbing the snow
    On the branches.

Hardly telling
The newer blue spruce branches
From the older ones . . .

On this shortest day,
  The evergreens pointing at the sun—
    The sun pointing back.

A golden bough
Of mistletoe blooming
On the dead oak.

Now clattering
In this winter wind,
Brown oak leaves.

A flitting shadow,
  From a vase of dried flowers,
    Falls on the young girl.

Below:
  Brown leaves rotting;
  Above—such stars!

Haiku Byways
Vol. I, No. 2

Wet, wild geese
   Riding each other's wing wind
      Northward.

The old man
   Comes too soon to gaze
     At plum blossoms . . .

Haiku Magazine
Vol. 4, No. 2/3

Picking up
This idle paintbrush
And sniffing the air . . .

Now thrown back
 Into the surge of the surf,
  The melting mists.